# WORLD HISTORY
### THE HUMAN EXPERIENCE

## Enrichment Activities

Mounir A. Farah
Andrea Berens Karls

**GLENCOE**
McGraw-Hill

New York, New York   Columbus, Ohio   Woodland Hills, California   Peoria, Illinois

## To the Teacher

*Enrichment Activities* extend and enrich a particular topic or theme for each chapter of *World History: The Human Experience*. The activities may be used at any time during chapter study or may be completed after students have taken and passed the chapter test.

Each one-page activity opens with an introduction and directions. It then provides students with an activity that requires them to analyze various presentations, including primary sources, maps, and graphs. Questions following the activity require students to apply the information they have read in the activity. The questions also allow students to practice critical thinking skills.

Answers to the activities are provided at the back of the booklet.

*Glencoe/McGraw-Hill*
A Division of The McGraw-Hill Companies

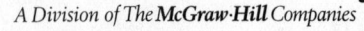

Copyright © by The McGraw-Hill Companies, Inc. All rights reserved. Permission is granted to reproduce the material contained herein on the condition that such material be reproduced only for classroom use; be provided to students, teachers, and families without charge; and be used solely in conjunction with *World History: The Human Experience*. Any other reproduction, for use or sale, is prohibited without prior written permission of the publisher.

Send all inquiries to:
Glencoe/McGraw-Hill
936 Eastwind Drive
Westerville, OH 43081

ISBN 0-02-823229-1

Printed in the United States of America
3 4 5 6 7 8 9 10   045   02 01 00 99 98

# ENRICHMENT ACTIVITIES

## TABLE OF CONTENTS

| | | |
|---|---|---|
| **To The Teacher** | | ii |
| **Acknowledgments** | | iv |
| **Chapter 1** | The Social Impact of Agriculture | 1 |
| **Chapter 2** | The Seasons of the Nile | 2 |
| **Chapter 3** | The Roots of English | 3 |
| **Chapter 4** | The Gods and Goddesses: A Family Tree | 4 |
| **Chapter 5** | Evidence for Women Poets: Sappho | 5 |
| **Chapter 6** | From Rome to Washington | 6 |
| **Chapter 7** | Planning and Describing Migrations | 7 |
| **Chapter 8** | *Panchatantra* Fables | 8 |
| **Chapter 9** | "Happy New Year!" Chinese Style | 9 |
| **Chapter 10** | Religious Faith Meets Nationalist Pride | 10 |
| **Chapter 11** | Ramadan | 11 |
| **Chapter 12** | The Noble Household | 12 |
| **Chapter 13** | Jerusalem: Bloodshed and Carnage | 13 |
| **Chapter 14** | History Reflected in Art | 14 |
| **Chapter 15** | The Mayan Belief System | 15 |
| **Chapter 16** | The State of the World, 1516 | 16 |
| **Chapter 17** | The European View of the Americas | 17 |
| **Chapter 18** | Islam in China | 18 |
| **Chapter 19** | Addressing the Troops | 19 |
| **Chapter 20** | The Commotion Galileo Caused | 20 |
| **Chapter 21** | The First American Hero | 21 |
| **Chapter 22** | The *Levée en Masse* | 22 |
| **Chapter 23** | Textile Workers and Managers in Fall River | 23 |
| **Chapter 24** | Please Advise! | 24 |
| **Chapter 25** | War and Violence | 25 |
| **Chapter 26** | Culture and Nationalism | 26 |
| **Chapter 27** | Famous Last Words | 27 |
| **Chapter 28** | Getting the Message Across | 28 |
| **Chapter 29** | No Laughing Matter: Interpreting Political Cartoons | 29 |
| **Chapter 30** | Salt and Satyagraha | 30 |
| **Chapter 31** | The Cost of War | 31 |
| **Chapter 32** | The Marshall Plan | 32 |
| **Chapter 33** | The Weight of War | 33 |
| **Chapter 34** | Education for Life | 34 |
| **Chapter 35** | A Single Region, Different Cultures | 35 |
| **Chapter 36** | Leaders of Modern-Day Latin American Resistance Movements | 36 |
| **Chapter 37** | The War in Bosnia | 37 |
| **Answer Key** | | 38 |

# ACKNOWLEDGMENTS

**Text**

**5** The Regents of the University of California, and Mary Barnard, for "Sleep, Darling" and "He Is More Than a Hero" from *Sappho; A New Translation*, University of California Press, copyright © 1958, renewed Mary Barnard 1984.

**11** From *The Seed and the Soil: Gender and Cosmology in Turkish Village Society* by Carol Delany, copyright © 1991 by the Regents of the University of California.

**13** From *Chronicles of the Crusades* by Joinville and Villehardouin, translated by M. R. B. Shaw, (Penguin Classics, 1963) copyright © by M. R. B. Shaw, 1963.

**15** From *A Forest of Kings: The Untold Story of the Ancient Maya* by Linda Schele and David Freidel, copyright © 1990 by Linda Schele and David Freidel.

**16** From *Utopia* by Sir Thomas More text and translation by Robert M. Adams.

**17** From *Essays* by Michel de Montaigne, translated by J. M. Cohen, copyright © 1958 by J. M. Cohen.

**19** From "Speech to the Troops at Tilbury" by Elizabeth I.

**20** From *Galileo* by Bertolt Brecht, translated by Charles Laughton, edited by Eric Bentley, copyright © 1940 by Arvid Englind, copyright © 1952 by Bertolt Brecht, copyright © 1966 by Eric Bentley.

**21** From "A Man on Horseback" by Richard Brookhiser, in *The Atlantic Monthly* Vol. 277 No. 1 (January 1996) copyright © 1995 by The Atlantic Monthly Company.

**22** From *War* by Gwynne Dyer, copyright © 1985 by Media Resources.

**23** From *Fall River, Lowell, and Lawrence: From the Thirteenth Annual Report of the Massachusetts Bureau of Statistics of Labor* by Carroll D. Wright, published 1882 by Rand, Avery and Co.

**24** From *How We Lived: A Documentary History of Immigrant Jews in America* by Irving Howe and Kenneth Libo, copyright ©1979 by Irving Howe and Kenneth Libo.

**25** From *On War* by Carl von Clausewitz, translation copyright © 1908 by Routledge and Kegan Paul, Ltd.

**30** From *Gandhi Wields the Weapon of Moral Power* by Gene Sharp, copyright © 1960 by The Navajivan Trust.

**33** From *The Things They Carried* by Tim O'Brien, copyright © 1990 by Tim O'Brien.

**34** From *So Long a Letter* by Mariama Bâ, translation copyright © 1981 by Modupé Bodé-Thomas.

**36** From "In His Own Words: Sandino's Autobiography" from *Nicaraguan Perspectives*. No. 16 (Winter 1988/89).
From *Revolution in Mexico: Years of Upheaval, 1910–1940*, edited by James W. Wilkie and Albert L. Michaels, published by Knopf, 1969.

**37** From *Outreach*, newsletter published by Women for Women in Bosnia, March 1996.

**Photographs**

**29** "Interrupting the Ceremony" copyrighted © Chicago Tribune Company. All rights reserved. Used with permission.

Name ................................................ Date ................................ Class ................................

# Enrichment Activity 1

## The Social Impact of Agriculture

Profound changes resulted from the shift from hunting and gathering to farming. Several of these changes and their social consequences are given in the table below. Study the table, then complete the assignment that follows.

| Change | Social Consequence |
| --- | --- |
| People lived in one place and no longer had to carry all their possessions. | People who could afford material goods began to accumulate them. |
| Farmers could grow more food than they needed to feed their families. | Farmers could barter surplus food for textiles, tools, and pottery made by artisans. |
| Land and water became valuable economic resources. | Leaders with armies arose to conquer large land areas. Rulers forced people who had no power to do hard jobs such as producing food and constructing irrigation systems. |
| Male warriors competed for land, water, and power. | Women lost the power they had shared in hunter-gatherer societies to male warriors who could protect them and their children. |

*Pretend that you were a witness to one of the changes shown above, and you experienced its social consequences. Write a journal entry describing your role in the society and your reaction to the change.*

_____
_____
_____
_____
_____
_____
_____
_____
_____
_____
_____
_____

*World History*              Enrichment Activities

Name ................................................................................................ Date ............................................... Class ...............................

# Enrichment Activity 2

## The Seasons of the Nile

*Ancient civilizations developed near rivers. When the rivers flooded, they deposited rich silt on the land, making it good farmland. Read the following selection about the flooding of the Nile and answer the questions that follow.*

The behavior of the Nile determined the seasons for farmers in ancient Egypt. There were really three seasons: inundation, receding waters, and drought. Inundation was the period during which the Nile flooded. Afterwards, the flood waters receded, withdrawing from the fields. Farmers plowed the land and planted their crops during this time. Drought was the dry period, when farmers harvested their crops.

Knowing in advance how much the Nile would flood was an important role of government, and much of the kings' power came from their ability to accurately predict the extent of the floods. Good flooding meant abundant harvests; a low flood could mean famine. As Egyptian civilization progressed, it became possible to move farther upstream to measure the source of flooding and get earlier information on the extent of the year's flood.

Egyptian farmers devised a series of dams, levees, and canals to control the flooding river. They built levees around villages to keep water out. They constructed earthen dams in fields after the flood to keep water in long enough to enrich the soil. They dug canals and then punctured the dams to allow water to flow into fields as needed. As a final method of irrigation, they carried water by hand to distant fields not reached by the floods.

The value of land—how heavily it was taxed—was determined by its proximity to the river. Lowland fields that flooded naturally were the most prized. Those farther inland that needed to be flooded through irrigation were taxed at a lower rate.

**1.** What is the main idea of the selection? _____
_____

**2.** From what you have read about Egyptian civilization, how necessary was an abundant labor force to prepare the fields for planting?
_____

**3.** Why do you think kings derived their power from their ability to predict the flood? _____
_____
_____

**4.** Why do you think land closer to the river was more valuable? _____
_____
_____

**5.** From what you have read about Egyptian religion, briefly describe the role water in general, and the Nile in particular, might have played in the religion of ancient Egypt.
_____
_____
_____

Name ................................................ Date ................................ Class ................................

# Enrichment Activity 3

## The Roots of English

English has drawn words from many languages. In fact, much of the richness of our language comes from the words we have borrowed from German, Spanish, French, Italian, and the Eastern languages. Read the passage explaining the history of the words *paradise* and *magic*. Then look at the list of words derived from Arabic below. Survey your friends to see how many of the words they can define. Check their answers in a dictionary.

The word *paradise* comes from an ancient Persian word for a pleasure garden or park filled with deer. Kings and satraps (provincial governors) often had such parks. The English word *magic* comes from the word *magus*, the ancient Persian word for a member of the mysterious Persian priestly clan. A magus was a person who knew a great deal about religion. Most likely, the magi were scribes and record keepers. The word *magic* may have assumed its present meaning from a group of the priestly clan who relocated to Babylonia and told fortunes. The three wise men from the east who journeyed to visit the infant Jesus were Persian magi.

| Word | Possible Meanings | Actual Meaning |
|---|---|---|
| albacore | | |
| algorithm | | |
| carafe | | |
| cipher | | |
| garble | | |
| hazard | | |
| henna | | |
| lute | | |
| marabout | | |
| quintal | | |
| saffron | | |
| saker | | |
| tarragon | | |

*World History*      Enrichment Activities    **3**

Name .................................................. Date ........................... Class ...................

# Enrichment Activity 4

## The Gods and Goddesses: A Family Tree

Anthropologists use what is known as a kinship chart to map how members of a family ("kin") are related to one another. A kinship chart is more commonly referred to as a family tree. The Greek deities were much like humans—they had parents and siblings just as we do. Study the kinship chart below to discover the family relationship of many of the most powerful gods and goddesses in the Greek religion, then use the chart to answer the questions that follow. Note that the equal signs join two parents, and the branches coming from them show their children.

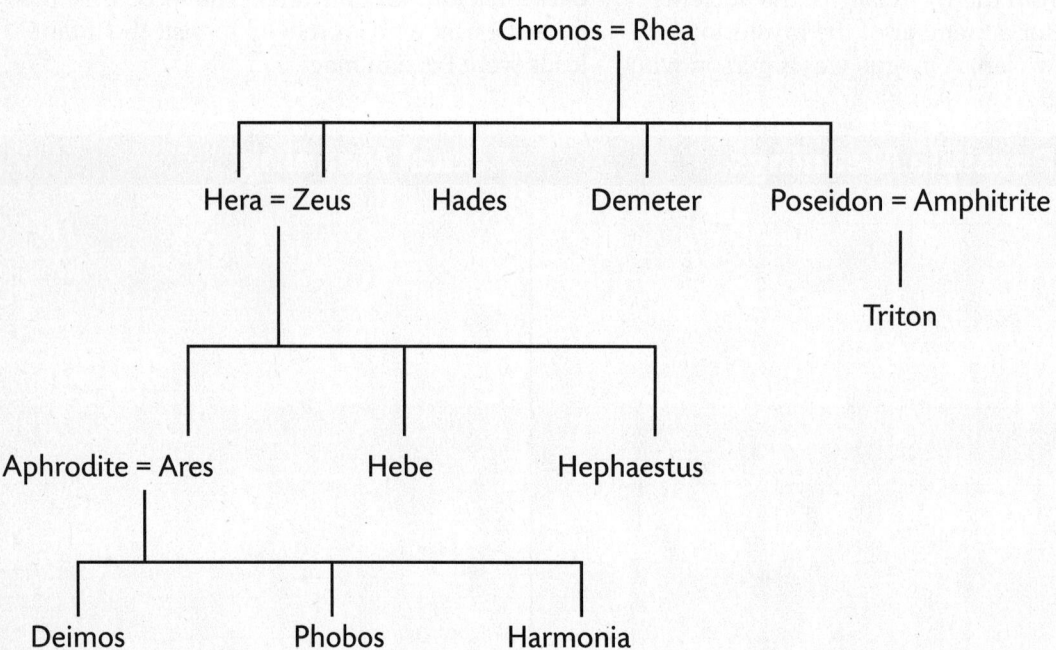

1. Who were Zeus's parents? _____

2. How many brothers and sisters did Zeus have? Who are they? _____

3. Who was Zeus's wife? _____

4. How many of Chronos and Rhea's grandchildren are shown in the chart? Who are they? _____
_____

5. How many of Chronos and Rhea's great-grandchildren are shown? Who are they? _____
_____

6. How are Ares and Triton related? _____

4  Enrichment Activities                                                World History

Name _____ Date _____ Class _____

# Enrichment Activity 5

## Evidence for Women Poets: Sappho

Although Athens was the home of some of the best-known poets during the Classical and Hellenistic periods, there is no record of Athenian women composing poetry. However, in city-states where the status of women was higher, women did write poetry. The best-known example was Sappho, who lived during the early sixth century B.C. Although little of her work has survived, she was so renowned for her skill that Plato later called her "the tenth muse." Use the poems below to discover the concerns and interests of this legendary poet.

### Sleep, darling

Sleep, darling

I have a small
daughter called
Cleis, who is

like a golden
flower

I wouldn't
take all Croesus'
kingdom with love
thrown in, for her

### He is more than a hero

He is more than a hero

He is a god in my eyes—
the man who is allowed
to sit beside you—he

who listens intimately
to the sweet murmur of
your voice, the enticing

laughter that makes my own
heart beat fast. If I meet
you suddenly, I can't

speak—my tongue is broken;
a thin flame runs under
my skin; seeing nothing,

hearing only my own ears
drumming, I drip with
sweat;
trembling shakes my body

and I turn paler than
dry grass. At such times
death isn't far from me

---

**1.** Whom is the first poem about? To whom is the second poem addressed? _____
_____

**2.** How would you describe the speaker's attitude toward Cleis? _____
_____

**3.** How would you describe the speaker's attitude toward the man spoken of in the second poem?
_____
_____

**4.** Which types of love do the two poems express? _____
_____
_____

**5.** Write your own poem after the style of Sappho. When writing your poem, be sure to notice the simple imagery, straightforward style, concise lines, and attention to the details of everyday life that have made Sappho's work endure through the ages.

World History                                                                                                    Enrichment Activities  5

Name ........................................................................... Date ..................... Class .....................

# Enrichment Activity 6

## From Rome to Washington

The founders of the United States wanted to inspire generations of future Americans by evoking the governments of Athens and the Roman Republic. Such inspiration is evident in the architecture of buildings such as the Capitol, the Supreme Court, the Lincoln and Jefferson Memorials, and the Library of Congress. The Capitol, in fact, is named after the Capitoline Hill in Rome, the highest of the city's seven hills and the site of the Capitol, the temple of Jupiter.

How does the government of the United States today compare to that of the Roman Republic? Use the chart below to list similarities and differences between the governments and influence of the United States and the Roman Republic. Then answer the question that follows.

| Characteristic | United States | Roman Republic |
|---|---|---|
| Branches of government | | |
| Voters | | |
| Citizenship | | |
| Executive leader | | |
| Territorial expansion | | |
| Military power | | |
| Religion | | |

Was the Roman Republic a good source of inspiration for the founders of the United States? Why or why not? Write your answer below.

_____
_____
_____
_____
_____

6   Enrichment Activities                                            World History

Name ................................................................................... Date ........................... Class ...........................

# Enrichment Activity 7

## Planning and Describing Migrations

> Chapter 7 describes the developments of African civilizations over a period of 3,000 years. These civilizations flourished as they experienced migrations, cultural diffusion, and innovation. Contact with other cultures came about through trade, war, and travel.

The Bantu people migrated from West Africa because the land they lived on grew less and less productive while the population continued to increase. The land was no longer able to support them, so many families decided to move in search of more space and better land. The Bantu migrations eventually carried people to the other side of the continent.

**1.** Imagine that you are living in a Bantu village and are a member of the village council. Food production seems to be decreasing each year and the council is meeting to discuss the food shortage problem. Write a brief speech in which you outline your arguments to the council surrounding this issue. Ask yourself: Is it a temporary problem? Can new farming techniques be developed? Can the farmland be redistributed so that more arable land can be used for farming? Should the village move? Should only a few families move? Do you want to move from a village where you have lived your entire life?

_____
_____
_____
_____
_____
_____
_____

**2.** In the end, the village council has decided that the only solution is to move to a new area. Develop a written plan for the village's migration. Start by thinking about the problems you will face. Where will you go? How will you get there? How will you protect yourselves?

_____
_____
_____
_____
_____
_____
_____

**3.** Migrations still take place today around the world. Individuals and families decide to migrate from where they live for reasons other than just food and overpopulation. On a separate sheet of paper, write an essay describing various reasons you think people decide to move or migrate. Support your ideas with details or examples you have heard or read about in the news. Keep in mind that a migration may take place within one's own country or to another country.

Name ........................................................ Date ................................ Class ................................

# Enrichment Activity 8

## *Panchatantra* Fables

Throughout history, many writers have used fables to teach the difference between right and wrong. Sometimes fables are written about animals who act like humans. The fables best known to Westerners are those by Aesop. Like those Greek fables, the *Panchatantra* is a famous set of Indian fables composed during the Gupta Empire. Before you begin this activity, reread pages 212–214 in your textbook. Then read the following excerpt from the *Panchatantra* and answer the questions that follow.

### "The Scholars who brought a Dead Lion to Life"

Four Brahmans once set upon a journey. Three were quite intelligent and scholarly; the fourth had common sense. In a forest, they came upon the bones of a dead lion. Immediately, the three intelligent scholars wanted to bring the lion back to life.

"I can assemble the bones and make a skeleton," said one.

"I can provide it with skin and flesh and blood," said another.

The third Brahman said, "Well, I can breathe life into it."

The fourth Brahman, Common Sense, was quiet until the third Brahman started to breathe life into the lion. At this point he stopped him, saying, "Look, if you give this lion life it will kill us all."

The other scholars were angry at Common Sense for doubting their combined efforts to bring the lion to life.

"All right, then," Common Sense replied, "just let me climb that tree over there before you bring the lion to life."

The third scholar gave the lion life, after which it rose and killed all three Brahmans. After waiting for the lion to move away, the fourth Brahman, whose sense had saved him, came down from the tree and went home.

**1.** Why do you think three of the Brahmans want to raise the lion from the dead?

_____

**2.** What do you think the moral (lesson of right and wrong) of this story is?

_____

**3.** The *Panchatantra* is divided into five books, each emphasizing a moral lesson: "Loss of Friends"; "The Winning of Friends"; "How to Deal with Enemies"; "Loss of Gains"; and "Ill-Considered Actions." Which of these books do you think the fable you just read came from and why?

_____

_____

**4.** Why might the Gupta Empire have wanted to support writers who wrote fables teaching people the difference between right and wrong?

_____

_____

**5.** On a separate sheet of paper, write a short fable of your own. Remember that fables teach lessons. To get started, think about a lesson you learned when you were young. Then rewrite it by turning the humans into animals in your fable.

8   Enrichment Activities                                                                                                   World History

Name ........................................................................................ Date ........................................ Class ........................

# Enrichment Activity 9

## "Happy New Year!" Chinese Style

In the United States, we measure years officially by recording how long it takes for the earth to revolve once around the sun. This method is called a solar calendar, and it corresponds accurately with the seasons of the year. However, in order to calculate the solar year, a scientist needs instruments to measure the angle of the sun as it shines on the earth. Since many ancient cultures lacked these instruments, they relied on a lunar calendar instead. Read the information below about the lunar calendar and answer the questions that follow.

A lunar calendar is based on the cycle of the moon's phases, which can be observed without the use of scientific instruments. According to the traditional Chinese calendar, the year is made up of 12 lunar months. A lunar month is about 29.5 days long. This is the time it takes for the moon to pass through a complete cycle of phases, from full moon to new moon to full moon.

A year made up of 12 lunar months is shorter than a solar year. After a few years, lunar and solar calendars are out of synchronization. To correct this, a "leap month" is periodically added to the Chinese lunar calendar. Even so, Chinese holidays do not fall on the same solar-calendar dates each year. For example, Chinese New Year can occur anytime between January 21 and February 19 on the solar calendar. By contrast, New Year's Day on the solar calendar is always January 1.

1. What is the difference in length between a solar year (365 days) and a non-leap lunar year?

    _____

2. How long is an "average solar month," one-twelfth of a solar year?

    _____

3. What is the difference between the length of an "average solar month" and the length of a lunar month?

    _____

4. Considering this difference, how many lunar months would pass before the lunar calendar was 30 days (approximately a lunar month) behind the solar calendar? Based on this, after how many lunar months should a leap month be added to the lunar calendar?

    _____

    _____

5. Although the Chinese calendar is still used for calculating the timing of holidays, the solar calendar is the official one used by government and commerce. Why do you think this is so?

    _____

    _____

    _____

World History                                                                                               Enrichment Activities    9

Name _____ Date _____ Class _____

# Enrichment Activity 10

## Religious Faith Meets Nationalist Pride

What we call the Eastern Orthodox Church is actually made up of several autonomous, or self-governing, national churches, each of which has its own patriarch. For example, in Russia there is the Russian Orthodox Church, and in Romania, the Romanian Orthodox Church. Throughout history, the establishment of an autonomous national church was a source of nationalist pride as well as political conflict. Look at the table and answer the questions that follow.

| Country | Members of Autonomous Orthodox Church | Total Population |
|---|---|---|
| Armenia | 3,343,846 | 3,557,284 |
| Bulgaria | 7,458,918 | 8,775,198 |
| Georgia | 4,351,737* | 5,725,972 |
| Greece | 10,434,560 | 10,647,511 |
| Macedonia | 1,446,867 | 2,159,503 |
| Romania | 16,238,831 | 23,198,330 |
| Russian Federation | 37,477,272 | 149,909,089 |
| Yugoslavia | 7,216,191 | 11,101,833 |

* Includes 3,721,881 Georgian Orthodox and 629,856 Russian Orthodox.

1. What would be an appropriate title for the table? _____
2. What is the total population of Greece? _____
3. Which two countries are almost entirely Orthodox? _____
4. a. What is the total number of Orthodox in Georgia? _____
   b. Among Georgians, about how many times greater is the Georgian Orthodox membership than the Russian Orthodox membership? _____
   c. The Russian Orthodox population makes up about what percentage of Georgia's total population? _____
5. The Russian Orthodox population in the Russian Federation makes up about what percentage of the total population? _____
6. About how many more Romanian Orthodox are there than Greek Orthodox? _____

Name ................................................................... Date ........................................ Class ........................................

# Enrichment Activity 11

## Ramadan

As you have read, fasting is one of the five pillars of Islam, and the month-long fast that occurs during the month of Ramadan is required of all adult Muslims. As the following passage explains, the fast begins each day at dawn, at the moment when "white thread becomes distinct from black thread," and does not end until sunset. Read the excerpt below and answer the questions that follow. Use a separate sheet of paper for your answers.

Ramazan [Ramadan] . . . is an occasion during which believers are thought to be closer to God. Ramazan is a month-long period of fasting, somewhat like Lent only more stringent. It is a time of atonement. It is the month in which the Qur'an was allegedly revealed to Muhammed. It is said: "When the noble time of Ramazan comes, the doors of heaven are opened, the doors of hell closed, and the devils tied down." In other words, people's souls are opened to God and closed to **şeytan** (devils); they are sustained by God as by food.

During Ramazan the faithful keep a fast (**oruç**). All day, from before sunrise to after sunset, one must abstain from food and drink. . . . It is also not permissible to smoke, take medicine, or chew gum; in other words, no substance may enter the body. One must be separated from those things which promote and sustain life in its material earthly form; fasting is a way to remind people of their dependence on God for these things. **Oruç** is felt to be a great **sevap** (good work) by which God is pleased; if faithfully performed, it is believed to bring a remission of sins.
—From *The Seed and the Soil* by Carol Delaney

1. Why do the followers of Islam believe they are brought closer to God through their long period of fasting?

2. How are the body and the soul, and the gates of heaven and hell, thought to mirror each other during the fast?

3. The twenty-sixth night of Ramadan is called the "Night of Determination." According to the Quran, it is on this night that God will decide the destiny of the entire world for the course of the following year. How does this night correspond to the objectives of the rest of the fast? Support your response with details from the passage.

4. Take a moment to consider all the food you consume on an average day. How would you feel if you had to undergo a month-long fast?

5. You may be surprised to learn that Ramadan is usually thought of by Muslims as a time of celebration. After a long day of fasting, a light meal is enjoyed by neighbors and friends. Why might Ramadan be considered a time of social solidarity and enjoyment rather than simply one of hardship?

Name _____  Date _____  Class _____

# Enrichment Activity 12

## The Noble Household

Section 2 describes the lives of the feudal lords and ladies and the living and working conditions of the peasants. One of the important roles at this time was the management of the household, a task often performed by a noblewoman. The description below gives an account of what that task could involve. Read the description, then complete the activities.

A feudal household could be quite large. Important nobles could have a household of as many as 200 people. This meant a lot of management. Some of the work had to be delegated to various people, such as those in charge of the preparation and serving of food and wine or the manufacture and maintenance of clothing and linens. These people, in turn, made sure that the work was done. In addition, enormous quantities of food had to be gathered and purchased. Guests had to be entertained by musicians and performers. Horses and livestock had to be overseen, and farm work carried out and supervised. Children needed to be cared for and educated. Rooms had to be cleaned and warmed. Often, a chapel operated as a church and was attended at least once a day. Letters to lords and vassals had to be written. Rents had to be collected.

1. Imagine that you are the noblewoman of a castle with a household of 50 people. Use the information above and from the textbook to imagine the tasks you have to complete in one day. Fill in the tasks on the following roster.

    4:30 A.M. Daybreak and church

    5:00 A.M. _____

    7:00 A.M. _____

    9:00 A.M. _____

    11:00 A.M. _____

    1:00 P.M. _____

    3:00 P.M. _____

    4:30 P.M. Sundown and church

    5:00 P.M. _____

    7:00 P.M. Bed

2. Imagine that you must provide dinner for your guests and your immediate household—about 15 people. Make a list of items you may need to collect. Think of all the places you may need to travel on your own estate and elsewhere to acquire these things. Make a note about where to get each item. The list is begun for you. Use an extra sheet of paper to continue your list.

| Item | Location |
|---|---|
| 4 loaves of bread | mill |
| small jug of cooking oil | market in town |
|  |  |

Enrichment Activities

World History: The Human Experience

Name _____ Date _____ Class _____

# Enrichment Activity 13

## Jerusalem: Bloodshed and Carnage

Section 1 describes the Crusades and their effects on Christians, Muslims, and Jews. The First Crusade, made up of Crusaders from various places in western Europe, entered Jerusalem in A.D. 1099. At this time, Jerusalem was inhabited mainly by Muslims and Jews.

The following passage by William of Tyre describes the forces of one of the leaders of the First Crusade, Duke Godfrey of Lorraine (in eastern France), who soon after was chosen as ruler of Jerusalem. Read the description and complete the activities that follow.

The duke and those who were with him then united their forces and, protected by their shields and helmets, swept hither and thither through the streets and squares of the city with drawn swords. Regardless of age and condition, they laid low, without distinction, every enemy encountered. Everywhere was frightful carnage, everywhere lay heaps of severed heads, so that soon it was impossible to pass or to go from one place to another except over the bodies of the slain. Already the leaders had forced their way by various routes almost to the center of the city and wrought unspeakable slaughter as they advanced. A host of people followed in their train, athirst for the blood of the enemy and wholly intent upon destruction.

—from *Chronicles of the Crusades*, ed. Jainville and Villehardouin.

1. Imagine you are one of the Crusaders entering the city of Jerusalem at this time after making the journey for two or three years from your home. You are wearing an outer garment of linked metal rings and have been battling to get into the city for two months. Around you are the old stone buildings and temples of the Holy City. Describe the sights, sounds, and actions of those around you. Include how you feel about what is occurring.

_____
_____
_____
_____
_____
_____

2. Imagine you are one of the inhabitants of the city. You can be an old man or woman, one of those defending the city, or even a child. Describe the sights, sounds, and actions of those around you as you flee the invaders.

_____
_____
_____
_____
_____
_____

*World History: The Human Experience*  Enrichment Activities  **13**

Name _____ Date _____ Class _____

# Enrichment Activity 14

## History Reflected in Art

Besides being appreciated for their beauty, works of art often reflect the social conditions under which they were produced. For historians of ancient or endangered cultures, artwork can provide valuable clues to people's traditions, lifestyles, and environments, especially in the absence of forms of writing. Read the passage about Montagnard textiles and answer the questions that follow.

> Most people living in Vietnam today are members of the Viet ethnic group. However, a small ethnic minority, possessing a different culture and lifestyle from the larger Viet group, still lives in the highlands. Known as the Montagnards, a French word meaning "mountain people," these migratory farmers have often been discriminated against by both ethnic Viets and French colonists alike.
>
> The Montagnards weave distinct patterns into the cloth they produce. Each design (for instance, an animal or a plant) corresponds to a certain part of their lives. By studying these patterns historians can gain a better view of complex cultures. Many Montagnard patterns depict images associated with processing rice for eating. Others represent natural phenomena such as colorful bird feathers, the beak of the toucan, water buffalo teeth, and cricket body parts. Still others represent plant products such as kapok. Kapok are the silky strands surrounding the seeds of Southeast Asian trees also known as kapoks. The fibers are used extensively in stuffing mattresses, life preservers, and sleeping bags. During the later twentieth century, Montagnard textile patterns representing planes and helicopters began to appear. These were accompanied by designs that mimic guns and men riding on horseback.

1. Based on the descriptions of early textile patterns, what conclusions can you draw about the Montagnards' traditional lifestyle? _____

    _____

2. What do you think the late-twentieth-century patterns represent? How are these patterns different from more traditional ones? What conclusions can be drawn about the changes in the Montagnards' lives during the twentieth century?

    _____

    _____

    _____

3. Create your own textile pattern representing a everyday object in your life. Then show it to classmates and see if they can guess the object your pattern represents. Why might people living 100 years in the future find your patterns of interest? What might they learn from your pattern?

    _____

    _____

Name _____ Date _____ Class _____

# Enrichment Activity 15

## The Mayan Belief System

In 1970, a young art teacher named Linda Schele visited Mexico as a tourist. She went to Palenque, planning to spend a couple of hours looking at some Maya ruins. Instead, she spent her entire vacation studying them. She went back to Mexico again and again, and today she is one of the foremost authorities on the meanings of the glyphs, or icons, of the Maya writing system. Read the passage below and answer the questions that follow.

The Maya conception of time, however was very different from our own. Our old adage, "He who does not know history is doomed to repeat it" might have been expressed by the Maya as "He who does not know history cannot predict his own destiny." The Maya believed in a past which has always returned, in historical symmetries—endless cycles repeating patterns already set into the fabric of time and space. By understanding and manipulating this eternal, cyclic framework of possibility, divine rulers hoped to create a favorable destiny for their people. But while the Maya ahauob [rulers] could know only the immediate results of the events they put into motion, we are gradually reclaiming the full scope of their historical accomplishments from the obscurity of the past.

Our challenge then is to interpret this history, recorded in their words, images, and ruins, in a manner comprehensible to the modern mind yet true to the Maya's perceptions of themselves. . . . History unlocks the humanity of the Maya in a way not possible by any other means, for it reveals not only what they did, but how they thought and felt about the nature of reality.

It is important that we acknowledge this history, because only then will a true picture of the Americas emerge. The American chronicle does not begin with the landing of Columbus or the arrival of the Pilgrims, but with the lives of Maya kings in the second century B.C. We who live in this part of the world inherit a written history two millennia old and as important to us as the history of the ancient Egyptians or the Chinese, a history equal in longevity to that of Europe or Asia.

—From *A Forest of Kings: The Untold Story of the Ancient Maya* by Linda Schele and David Freidel

**1.** Why did the Maya think it was important to record their history?

_____

_____

**2.** What do Linda Schele and David Freidel hope to accomplish through their study of Maya ruins?

_____

_____

**3.** What do the authors mean by the "American chronicle" beginning in the second century B.C.?

_____

_____

**4.** Do you agree or disagree that it is important to understand the history of the Maya? Explain your answer on a separate sheet of paper.

*World History*        Enrichment Activities    **15**

Name ........................................................................................ Date ........................................ Class ........................................

# Enrichment Activity 16

## The State of the World, 1516

Section 2 describes the way northern Europe was affected by the Renaissance and humanist ideas. The following excerpt from Sir Thomas More's *Utopia* (1516) shows the author's critical vision of the state of Europe at this time. Read the excerpt and answer the questions that follow. Use a separate sheet of paper.

When I run over in my mind the various commonwealths flourishing today, so help me God, I can see in them nothing but a conspiracy of the rich, who are fattening up their own interests under the name and title of the commonwealth. They invent ways and means to hang onto whatever they have acquired by sharp practice, and then they scheme to oppress the poor by buying up their toil and labor as cheaply as possible. These devices become law as soon as the rich, speaking through the commonwealth—which, of course, includes the poor as well—say they must be observed.

And yet when these insatiably greedy and evil men have divided among themselves goods which would have sufficed for the entire people, how far they remain from the happiness of the Utopian Republic, which has abolished not only money but with it greed! What a mass of trouble was cut away by that one step! What a thicket of crimes was uprooted! Everyone knows that if money were abolished, fraud, theft, robbery, quarrels, brawls, seditions, murders, treasons, poisonings, and a whole set of crimes which are avenged but not prevented by the hangman would at once die out. If money disappeared, so would fear, anxiety, worry, toil, and sleepless nights. Even poverty, which seems to need money more than anything else, would vanish if money were entirely done away with.

Consider if you will this example. Take a barren year of failed harvests, when many thousands of men have been carried off by hunger. If at the end of the famine the barns of the rich were searched, I dare say positively enough grain would be found in them to have kept all those who died of starvation and disease from even realizing that a shortage ever existed—if only it had been divided equally among them. So easily might men get the necessities of life if that cursed money, which is supposed to provide access to them, were not in fact the chief barrier to our getting what we need to live. Even the rich, I'm sure, understand this. They must know that it's better to have enough of what we really need than an abundance of superfluities, much better to escape from our many present troubles than to be burdened with great masses of wealth.

1. Compare the quote from Erasmus on page 414, in which he criticizes the popes for their corruption, with the excerpt above. How are they similar? How are they different?

2. Compare the description of commonwealths in More's time with society today. How are they similar? How is society different today?

3. Put yourself in the place of a rich person and argue in favor of a commonwealth. Then put yourself in the place of a poor peasant and argue in favor of a utopia.

Name _____ Date _____ Class _____

# Enrichment Activity 17

## The European View of the Americas

As European explorers made discoveries on their ocean voyages, many writers began to consider the proper way to relate to new people and different ways of life. A lawyer by profession, Michel Montaigne (1533–1592) retired to his estate in the Bordeaux region of France in 1571 to write a collection of essays that was first published in 1580. In his *Essais*, Montaigne gives his personal opinion on a range of issues of the day. Read the following excerpts from his essay "On Cannibals," then answer the questions that follow.

I had with me for a long time a man who had lived ten or twelve years in that other world which has been discovered in our time, in the place where Villegaignon landed [Brazil], and which he called Antarctic France. This discovery of so vast a country seems to me worth reflecting on. I should not care to pledge myself that another may not be discovered in the future, since so many greater men than we have been wrong about this one. I am afraid that our eyes are bigger than our stomachs, and that we have more curiosity than understanding. We grasp at everything, but catch nothing except wind. . . .

I do not believe, from what I have been told about this people, that there is anything barbarous or savage about them, except that we call barbarous anything that is contrary to our own habits. Indeed we seem to have no other criterion of truth and reason than the type and kind of opinions and customs current in the land where we live. There we always see the perfect religion, the perfect political system, the perfect and most accomplished way of doing everything.

**1.** Why does Montaigne hesitate to guess whether there are additional new countries to be discovered?

_____

**2.** How might Montaigne's observation that "our eyes are bigger than our stomachs" be related to the European conquest of the Americas?

_____

**3.** How does Montaigne characterize the people who live in the Americas?

_____

**4.** In what does Montaigne find fault with the way Europeans perceive their own social customs?

_____

**5.** Ethnocentrism is the attitude that one's own ethnic group, culture, or nation is superior to all others. It is the belief that one has the best religion, the best political system, and the most accomplished way of doing things. How far have people come since Montaigne's time in acknowledging and exploring other people's "differences" as potentially equal or superior to their own?

_____

_____

_____

_____

World History — Enrichment Activities

Name _____  Date _____  Class _____

# Enrichment Activity 18

## Islam in China

You have read about the spread of Islam throughout the Middle East and the various social and political systems that evolved from it. For example, there are Suleiman's *millets* and the religious advisory board he established known as the Ulema. Read the selection below and then answer the questions that follow. You will need to use the information you learned in Chapter 18 to link events in China with the information below.

Chinese Muslims are either descendants of Turkic people from Central Asia or descendants of Chinese converts to Islam. Islam probably reached China along trade routes and grew slowly. When the Mongols overthrew the Song dynasty, they established the Yuan dynasty. This period has been called the "golden age" of Islam in China. Under the Yuan dynasty, Muslims received special status, including the right to hold powerful state positions. By 1368, the Mongols had been overthrown and the Ming dynasty was in power. The Muslims lost their special status and government positions. When the Qing dynasty came to power, the status of Muslims was lower than it had been before. As a result, the Muslims rebelled, most notably in the Panthay Rebellion. This rebellion lasted from 1855 to 1873, when it was finally crushed.

1. From what you know of Muslim trade routes, how do you think Islam reached China in the first place? Based on this information, where would you expect Muslim communities to be located? (Review Chapter 14)

   _____
   _____
   _____

2. How can you explain the length of the Panthay Rebellion, based on what you know of the state of the Qing dynasty during the nineteenth century?

   _____
   _____
   _____

3. Based on the structure of Chinese dynasties, why would Islam have been persecuted by the Ming and Qing dynasties? (Hint: Think about the Confucian order system.)

   _____
   _____
   _____

4. How did the Qing and Ming repression of Muslims differ from Akbar's religious policies in India?

   _____
   _____
   _____

Enrichment Activities                                      World History

Name _____ Date _____ Class _____

# Enrichment Activity 19

## Addressing The Troops

By 1558, when Elizabeth Tudor ascended to the throne of England at the age of 25, she could read and write Greek, Latin, French, Italian, Spanish, German, and, of course, English. During the era that was named for her, she was celebrated in many poems and plays. Her own writing, however, reveals the same intelligence and learning that distinguished much of sixteenth-century writing.

Below is the speech that Elizabeth delivered to the British troops assembled at Tilbury in 1588 waiting for the landing of the Spanish Armada. Read the speech, then answer the questions that follow.

---

My loving people,

We have been persuaded by some that are careful of our safety, to take heed how we commit our selves to armed multitudes, for fear of treachery; but I assure you I do not desire to live to distrust my faithful and loving people. Let tyrants fear, I have always so behaved myself that, under God, I have placed my chiefest strength and safeguard in the loyal hearts and good-will of my subjects; and therefore I come amongst you, as you see, at this time, not for my recreation and disport, but being resolved, in the midst and heat of the battle, to live or die amongst you all; to lay down for my God, and for my kingdom, and my people, my honour and my blood, even in the dust. I know I have the body but of a weak and feeble woman; but I have the heart and stomach of a king, and king of England too, and think foul scorn that Parma or Spain, or any prince of Europe, should dare to invade the borders of my realm; to which rather than any dishonour shall grow by me, I myself will take up arms, I myself will be your general, judge, and rewarder of every one of your virtues in the field. I know already, for your forwardness you have deserved rewards and crowns; and We do assure you in the word of a prince, they shall be duly paid you. In the mean time, my lieutenant general shall be in my stead, than whom prince never commanded a more noble or worthy subject; not doubting but by your obedience to my general, by your concord in the camp, and your valour in the field, we shall shortly have a famous victory over those enemies of my God, of my kingdom, and of my people.

---

1. According to Elizabeth, why is she at Tilbury with the troops? _____

2. What does Elizabeth's presence at Tilbury with the soldiers tell you about her character? _____

3. How would you describe the tone or mood of this speech? _____

4. What effect do you think this speech had on the soldiers? _____

5. Imagine that Philip II of Spain was addressing his troops as they set off to invade England. How do you think his speech might be the same as Elizabeth's? How might it be different?

_____

World History                                              Enrichment Activities    19

# Enrichment Activity 20

## The Commotion Galileo Caused

In Chapter 20, you read about the reaction of the Catholic Church to Galileo's ideas, which conflicted with Church teachings. Galileo's hypothesis that the earth was not the center of the universe threatened to undermine the religious world-view that pervaded every aspect of European society. Read the excerpt below from Bertolt Brecht's play *Galileo*, then complete the activity that follows.

*Around the corner from the market place a* BALLAD SINGER *and his* WIFE, *who is costumed to represent the earth in a skeleton globe made of thin bands of brass, are holding the attention of a sprinkling of representative citizens, some in masquerade, who were on their way to see the carnival procession. From the market place the noise of an impatient crowd.*

BALLAD SINGER (*accompanied by his* WIFE *on the guitar*):
When the Almighty made the universe
He made the earth and then he made the sun.
Then round the earth he bade the sun to turn—
That's in the Bible, Genesis, Chapter One.
And from that time all beings here below
Were in obedient circles meant to go:
    Around the pope the cardinals
    Around the cardinals the bishops
    Around the bishops the secretaries
    Around the secretaries the aldermen
    Around the aldermen the craftsmen
    Around the craftsmen the servants
    Around the servants the dogs, the chickens, and the beggars.

*A conspicuous reveller—henceforth called the* SPINNER—*has slowly caught on and is exhibiting his idea of spinning around. He does not lose dignity, he faints with mock grace.*

BALLAD SINGER:
Up stood the learned Galileo
Glanced briefly at the sun
And said: "Almighty God was wrong
In Genesis, Chapter One!"
    Now that was rash, my friends, it is no matter small:
    For heresy will spread today like foul diseases.
    Change Holy Writ, forsooth? What will be left at all?
    Why: each of us would say and do just what he pleases!

**1.** Write a one-sentence summary of the message the Ballad Singer tries to convey.
_____
_____

**2.** Write your own ballad, poem, or short play about either Copernicus or Diderot and the persecution either man faced for expressing his views. If necessary, use a separate sheet of paper.
_____
_____
_____
_____
_____
_____
_____

# Enrichment Activity 21

## The First American Hero

George Washington retains such an imposing position in American history that we are sometimes blinded by the myth and no longer see the real man. Even in his own day, Washington was greatly admired by those around him. Recently, historian Richard Brookhiser described Washington's heroic qualities. Read the passage below. Then on a separate sheet of paper answer the questions that follow.

The list of personal events and traits that enabled George Washington to do what he did is long and various, and ranges from a youthful bout of smallpox, which immunized him against the disease, to a fondness for the Stoic philosopher Seneca, which may have immunized him against temper tantrums. But the important qualities that shaped Washington fall into only a few categories. His character may be described as a three-story building. The top floor was furnished with the political ideas of eighteenth-century America, with which we are familiar. But the other two stories were equally important. The second floor was his morals.... The ground floor consisted of what was given to him by nature and cultivated by the conditions of his life: his physicality and his temperament. His form was imposing, and his temper was dangerous. Displaying the one and controlling the other were essential to his success as a leader....

... One English visitor wrote in 1796, "Washington has something uncommonly majestic and commanding in his walk, his address, his figure, and his countenance." It was an impression not of glamour, or of beauty—some of his features (the large hands, the shallow chest) were potentially unattractive—but of the presence of the whole figure. Many of us have bodies that sit or stand dully, or droop like suits on wire hangers. Washington's organized the space around it, as a dancer's arms or legs seem to stretch beyond the tips of the fingers or toes.

Soldiers were very much aware of his presence and his doings. James Thacher, a medical officer of the American Army, wrote that when Washington first took command, in 1775, the men were "much gratified" to be able to pick him out from among his aides at a glance. The Marquis de Lafayette's rapturous description of him at the Battle of Monmouth Courthouse, even after making allowance for hero worship, explains why Washington's men considered him heroic: "His graceful bearing on horseback, his calm and deportment which still retained a trace of displeasure ... were all calculated to inspire the highest degree of enthusiasm. ... I thought then as now that I had never beheld so superb a man."

1. The author says that part of Washington's character was "furnished with the political ideas of eighteenth-century America." In two or three sentences, describe what the political ideas of eighteenth-century America were in regard to such things as government, personal liberties, and rights and freedoms.

2. The author also says that Washington's "form was imposing, and his temper was dangerous." Why do you think those two attributes would make Washington a successful military—and later, political—leader?

3. Until the twentieth century, American heroes were people in public life, often military leaders, and almost always men. Changes in American culture have created heroes in all walks of life. Identify someone who is a hero to you, and identify at least three attributes of your hero that you find appealing and list the reasons why.

*World History* — Enrichment Activities

# Enrichment Activity 22

## The *Levée en Masse*

Four months after the French revolutionaries proclaimed the first day of the "Year I of Liberty," they faced fierce attacks from European monarchies that feared the spread of the revolution. Desperate, the leaders of the revolution made a decision that would change the face of warfare forever. Read the excerpt below and answer the questions that follow.

Almost all of the monarchies of Europe launched their armies against France to stamp out the sacrilegious revolutionaries, and when what was left of the old royal army, aided by volunteers, proved unable to stem the attacks, the National Convention decided on conscription: the *levée en masse*.

. . . the convention issued the call for a *levée en masse* in August [1793]. By New Year's Day, 1794, the French armies numbered about 777,000 men, and the wars of mass armies that ensued ravaged Europe for the next two decades.

Conscription was not an entirely new idea . . . but it had never really amounted to more than compulsory selection of an unfortunate minority, nor had it lasted long or been extended to an entire country. But the French Revolution, with its principles of liberty and equality, first stimulated and then exploited a fervent nationalism which made conscription acceptable. It also made French troops behave differently.

The "nation in arms" produced poorly trained soldiers . . . who had no time to master the intricate drill of close-order formations, but their enthusiasm and numbers made up for it: attacking in clouds of skirmishers and disorderly columns, they often simply overwhelmed their better-trained adversaries. . . . Battles rarely ended in draws any more—Carnot of the Committee of Public Safety instructed the French armies in 1794 "to act in mass formations and take the offensive. . . . Give battle on a large scale and pursue the enemy until he is utterly destroyed."

The basic principle underlying all this was that whereas the prerevolutionary regular soldiers had been scarce and expensive, the lives of conscripts were plentiful and cheap. The disdain for casualties grew even greater once Napoleon had seized control of France in 1799. "You cannot stop me," he boasted to Count Metternich, the Austrian diplomat. "I spend thirty thousand men a month." It was not an idle boast: the losses of France in 1793–1814 amounted to 1.7 million dead—almost all soldiers—out of a population of 29 million.

—From *War* by Gwynne Dyer

1. Why did French revolutionary leaders institute the *levée en masse*? _____

2. How did the *levée en masse* change the French armies? _____

3. What "basic principle" does the author refer to? _____

4. France's enemies were reluctant to introduce conscription. Why do you think this was so?

5. What do you think about Napoleon's statement? How do you think this reflects on him?

Name ........................................................................................ Date ................................................. Class ............................................

# Enrichment Activity 23

## Textile Workers and Managers in Fall River

Section 4 describes the bleak conditions suffered by British and American textile workers during the 1800s. Relations between textile workers and managers, generally characterized by hostility, were particularly strained in the factories of Fall River, Massachusetts. The statements below were made by factory officers in Fall River to the Massachusetts Bureau of Statistics of Labor after persistent labor troubles in the mills prompted a state investigation in the 1880s. Read the statements and complete the activity that follows.

> [One] treasurer said further, "The discontent among the Fall River operatives [factory workers] is the outgrowth of the abnormal increase of the mills in 1871. We have the scum of the English and Irish in our midst; they brought their antagonistic notions with them. We never employ a man who belongs to a trades union if we know it; we root them out whenever we find them." . . . Another treasurer said, "there are plenty of complaints all the time. Last August the spinners protested against the 'twist' we insisted should be given the yarn, as it somewhat reduced their wages, and their cry was, 'Take out the drag.' They are never content unless they are complaining; now they complain because we have a 'sampler' who examines each bale of cotton we purchase in order to ascertain if it is like the sample."

1. To what does the first treasurer attribute the labor problems in the Fall River factories?
_____

2. What do you think is the meaning and significance of the "twist" and "sampler"?
_____
_____
_____

3. What do you think the workers meant by "Take out the drag"?
_____
_____

4. Write a likely statement given by a factory worker in response to one of the treasurers' testimonies.
_____
_____
_____

*World History*  Enrichment Activities  **23**

Name ................................................................................................ Date .................................................. Class ..................................

# Enrichment Activity 24

## Please Advise!

During the 1800s and early 1900s, immigrants who came to American cities seeking a better life found new problems. Overcrowded housing, exploitive working conditions, and an unfamiliar language were perhaps the worst of these. Equally troubling, however, was the destruction of old patterns and rules for living. A newspaper called the *Jewish Daily Forward* offered advice to Eastern European immigrants trying to create a new life in a new land. For example, in the old country, matchmakers and parents told young people whom to marry. In the new land, things were not so clear. Read the letter below that was written to the editor of the *Forward*. Then answer the questions that follow.

> I am a girl sixteen years old. I live together with my parents and two older sisters. Last year I met a young man. We love one another. He is a very respectable young man, and makes a fine living. My sisters have no fiancés. I know that should I marry they will never talk to me. My parents are also strongly against it since I am the youngest child. I do not want to lose my parents' love, and neither do I want to lose my [beloved] because this would break my heart. Give me some advice, dear Editor! What shall I do? Shall I leave my parents and marry my sweetheart, or shall I stay with my parents and lose the happiness of my life? Give me some advice, dear Editor!

1. What does the writer offer as reasons why she should marry this young man?
   _____
   _____

2. What are the reasons why the writer feels she cannot marry this young man?
   _____
   _____

3. What advice would you offer?
   _____
   _____

4. Would a sixteen-year-old girl whose family had lived in the United States for several generations face a dilemma like this one today? Why or why not?
   _____
   _____
   _____

5. On a separate sheet of paper, write a letter describing a personal problem an American teenager might face today. Then, list two ways the problem described in your letter is similar to the problem in the letter above and two ways that it is different.

24  Enrichment Activities  World History

Name ........................................................................... Date ..................................... Class .........................

# Enrichment Activity 25

## War and Violence

As the French and Indian, Crimean, and Franco-Prussian wars well illustrate, the violence of warfare became a common concern in the 1700s and 1800s. In fact, after retiring as an officer from the army of one of France's greatest enemies, the Prussian soldier Carl von Clausewitz (1780–1831) wrote a book on the philosophy of war titled simply *On War*, from which the following passage is taken. Use the passage to answer the questions below.

> We shall not enter into any of the abstruse definitions of War used by publicists. We shall keep to the element of the thing itself, to a duel. War is nothing but a duel on an extensive scale. If we would conceive as a unit the countless number of duels which make up a War, we shall do so best by supposing to ourselves two wrestlers. Each strives by physical force to compel the other to submit to his will: each endeavours to throw his adversary, and thus render him incapable of further resistance.
>
> War therefore is an act of violence intended to compel our opponent to fulfil our will.
>
> Violence arms itself with the inventions of Art and Science in order to contend against violence. Self-imposed restrictions, almost imperceptible and hardly worth mentioning, termed usages of International Law, accompany it without essentially impairing its power. Violence, that is to say, physical force (for there is no moral force without the conception of States and Law), is therefore the *means*; the compulsory submission of the enemy to our will is the ultimate *object*.

1. In the opening paragraph, to what does Clausewitz compare war? To what does he compare the two opponents in a war?
   _____
   _____

2. What is the role of art and science in warfare, according to Clausewitz?
   _____
   _____

3. How effective does Clausewitz think international law is in preventing violence?
   _____
   _____

4. How does Clausewitz define war? Explain whether you agree or disagree with his definition.
   _____
   _____

5. How does Clausewitz's definition of war hold up today? Survey at least five people to see how they define war. On a separate sheet of paper, write a paragraph comparing the views of the people surveyed with that of Clausewitz.

World History                                                                                           Enrichment Activities    **25**

Name .................................................................................... Date .................................... Class ....................

# Enrichment Activity 26

## Culture and Nationalism

Although nationalists often claim that the unification of national or linguistic groups is "natural" or "right," the nationalist movements of the 1800s and early 1900s actually "unified" a number of groups with distinct languages, religions, and economic lifestyles. Read the passage below and then complete the Venn diagrams that follow. Put the information that is the same for two or more regions in the areas of the circles that overlap. Put the information that is unique for a region in the area of the circle that does not overlap.

Before the unification, the areas that would become Italy included the Kingdom of the Two Sicilies, Lombardy, Piedmont, Venetia, and the Papal States. Although the dialects varied from region to region, the people throughout these regions spoke Italian. Most people were Catholic. The northern regions had an economy based on industry, while the southern regions were agricultural.

The peoples in the region that would become Germany were more varied. People in Prussia spoke German, and most were Protestants. Their economy was based on industry. In Schleswig, some people spoke German and others spoke Danish. Both language groups were Protestant. The economy was based mainly on agriculture. The southern German regions were home to Catholics who spoke German. Their economy was largely agricultural.

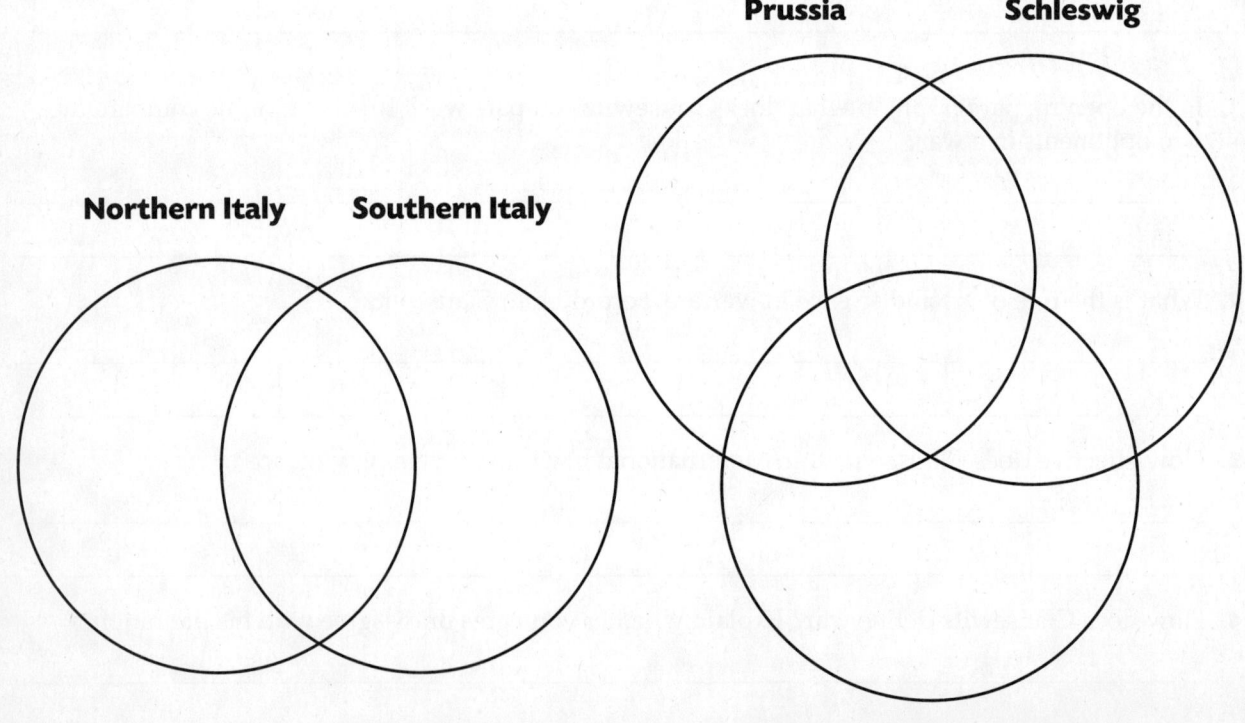

Diagram 1　　　　　　　　　　　　　　Diagram 2

26　Enrichment Activities　　　　　　　　　　　　　　World History

Name ................................................................................ Date ............................................... Class ...............................

# Enrichment Activity 27

## Famous Last Words

Historical figures are sometimes remembered for their last words spoken before dying. Read the following passage. Then write some likely last words for each of the following explorers, politicians, and writers listed below from Chapter 27. Be sure each person's last words reveal something about his or her character or history.

One of the people of the Age of Imperialism who gained great wealth was Cecil Rhodes, the South African explorer, statesman, and businessman. Rhodes made a fortune from mining gold and diamonds in southern Africa. Rhodes then went on to establish a South African colony and named it after himself: Rhodesia. The country is now known as Zimbabwe. On his deathbed in 1902, Rhodes is reputed to have said: "So little done—so much to do."

Other famous figures of the day departed with equally characteristic words. British explorer Lawrence Oates, noted for his composure under pressure, walked to his death in 1912 in an attempt to help his companions. They were starving to death during an expedition to the North Pole. As he left, Oates said: "I am just going outside and I may be some time." Ludwig van Beethoven, the German composer who was deaf for the last 29 years of his life, died in 1827, saying, "I shall hear in heaven." Self-assured General John Sedgwick, Union commander in the Civil War, was killed at the Battle of Spotsylvania Courthouse, Virginia, in 1864. He was shot while looking over a balcony at the enemy lines and saying: "They couldn't hit an elephant at this dist—."

1. Rudyard Kipling _____
2. Henry M. Stanley _____
3. King Leopold II of Belgium _____
4. Ferdinand de Lesseps _____
5. Theodore Roosevelt _____
6. Empress Ci Xi _____
7. Sun Yat-sen _____
8. James Monroe _____
9. Pancho Villa _____
10. Porfirio Díaz _____

World History                                                                                    Enrichment Activities    **27**

Name _____ Date _____ Class _____

# Enrichment Activity 28

## Getting the Message Across

Governments often use methods of propaganda or persuasion to get their citizens to side with the government's policies at a given time, especially during times of war. Governments use the media as an easy way to distribute their message. Today these methods include television ads, print ads, or radio spots. In the era before television was invented, governments used posters to carry their propagandistic messages. During World War I, governments from both the Allies and the Central Powers used illustrated posters to rally their citizens behind their war cause. Read the following description of a poster that appeared in 1917. Then answer the questions that follow.

An American wartime poster from 1917 shows a smiling, gray-haired woman standing in front of an American flag. Her arms are open and her hands are outstretched. She is depicted as a homey and maternal woman, almost grandmotherly in appearance. In the background, the artist has depicted various battle scenes in miniature. The poster reads, "Women! Help America's Sons Win the War. Buy U.S. Government Bonds."

1. To whom do you think this poster is addressed?
   _____

2. What is the persuasive point of the poster?
   _____

3. Why do you think the artist drew the woman as a smiling, gray-haired, grandmotherly type?
   _____

4. Why do you think the woman's hands are outstretched?
   _____

5. To what emotions do you think the artist is trying to appeal?
   _____

6. Why do you think the artist has drawn the battle scenes in the background rather than the foreground?
   _____

7. Design your own wartime poster. Pick a clearly stated goal, such as asking volunteers to join the army or suggesting that people not waste food during the wartime shortages. Find other examples of posters in library reference books to help you. In drawing the poster, be sure that it will grab people's attention and convey your message clearly and persuasively. What is the content of your message? What persuasive techniques do you want to use? To which emotions do you wish to appeal?

Name .................................................. Date .................. Class ..............

# Enrichment Activity 29

## No Laughing Matter: Interpreting Political Cartoons

Whether you are reading today's newspaper or researching history, political cartoons can help you understand the arguments surrounding an issue. Cartoonists illustrate their point of view through satirical drawings rather than lengthy editorials. Sometimes their cartoons depict actual people involved in an issue; other times the characters symbolize ideas, groups, or nations. Look at the following political cartoon and answer the questions that follow to help you to understand its meaning.

1. What type of ceremony is being depicted by the cartoon?
   _____
   _____

2. Who is the bearded man, and what does he represent?
   _____
   _____

3. What does the woman represent?
   _____
   _____

4. What does the ceremony symbolize?
   _____
   _____

5. What is interrupting the ceremony?
   _____
   _____

6. Why is the ceremony being interrupted?
   _____

7. Around what year might this cartoon have appeared?
   _____

8. Where do you think the cartoonist stands on this issue? Why do you think so?
   _____
   _____
   _____
   _____

*World History*        Enrichment Activities   **29**

Name _____ Date _____ Class _____

# Enrichment Activity 30

## Salt and Satyagraha

In 1930, when Gandhi returned to political life, *The New York Times* wrote, "In England the India crisis is not yet a topic of general conversation outside of political groups, and in India itself millions of people know nothing about it." Gandhi faced the problem of bringing the Indian struggle for independence to the attention of the world. He decided to do this through a protest on the salt tax. Read Gandhi's explanation of his protest, then answer the questions that follow.

There is no article like salt outside water by taxing which the State can reach even the starving millions, the sick, the maimed and the utterly helpless. The tax constitutes therefore the most inhuman poll tax that the ingenuity of man can devise. The . . . tax [raises the price by as much as] 2,400 per cent [over the wholesale] price! What this means to the poor can hardly be imagined by us. Salt production like cotton growing has been centralized for the sake of sustaining the inhuman monopoly. . . . The necessary consequence of salt monopoly was the . . . closing down of salt works in thousands of places where the poor people manufactured their own salt.

The illegality is in a Government that steals the people's salt and makes them pay heavily for the stolen article. The people, when they become conscious of their power, will have every right to take possession of what belongs to them.

—From February 27th issue of *Young India*

1. Write a one-sentence summary of Gandhi's explanation.

2. Explain why Gandhi chose the salt tax as the focus of his campaign.

3. In another statement, Gandhi said, "The salt tax oppresses all alike—Hindu, Mohammedan, Parsee, Christian, Jew." Why would this aspect of the tax make it a good focus for Gandhi's campaign?

4. What, according to Gandhi, made the tax on salt illegal?

5. The legitimacy of the salt tax campaign was strengthened by the fact that many British officials had also criticized the salt tax as unfair. Thus Gandhi and others were able to quote British officials in their campaigns against the tax. How might this have affected the initial response of the British government to the campaign?

6. The word *satyagraha* means "truth force." How was the force of truth used in the campaign against the salt tax?

Name _____ Date _____ Class _____

# Enrichment Activity 31

## The Cost of War

During the two world wars that took place between 1914 and 1945, more than 23,000,000 soldiers lost their lives. Look at the pie graphs below and answer the questions that follow.

**MILITARY DEATHS**

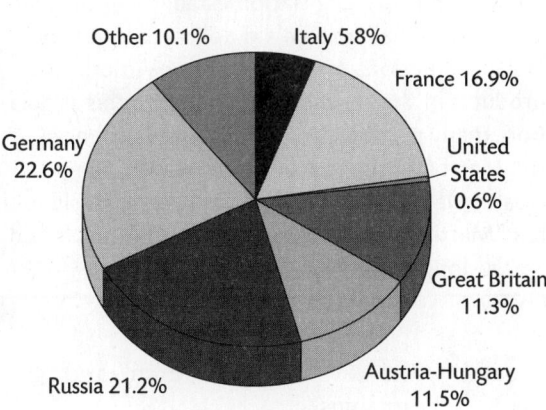

World War I
- Other 10.1%
- Italy 5.8%
- France 16.9%
- United States 0.6%
- Great Britain 11.3%
- Austria-Hungary 11.5%
- Russia 21.2%
- Germany 22.6%

TOTAL: 8,020,780

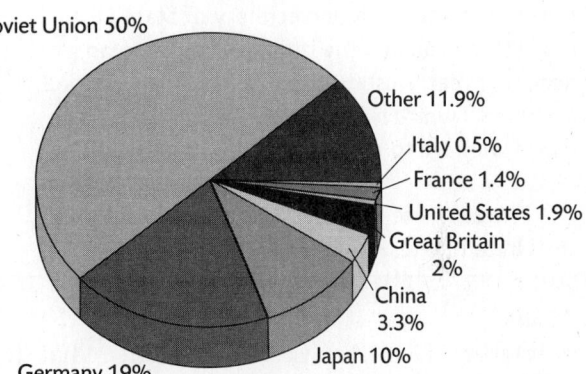

World War II
- Soviet Union 50%
- Other 11.9%
- Italy 0.5%
- France 1.4%
- United States 1.9%
- Great Britain 2%
- China 3.3%
- Japan 10%
- Germany 19%

TOTAL: 15,000,000

1. Based on the total number of military deaths, World War II was almost how many times as costly as World War I?
   _____

2. a. Which nation lost the most soldiers in World War II? _____
   b. About how many soldiers did this country lose? _____
   c. This country mobilized 20,000,000 troops. Military deaths make up what percentage of the total force mobilization?
   _____

3. a. About how many German soldiers were killed in World War II? _____
   b. Is this number greater or less than the number of Germans killed during World War I?

4. In which war did the United States lose more soldiers? _____

5. a. About how many French soldiers were killed during World War I?
   _____
   b. About how many were killed in World War II? _____
   c. Based on your knowledge of the two wars, why did the French lose fewer soldiers in World War II?
   _____
   _____

6. Military deaths among the Axis powers made up what percentage of the total deaths in World War II?
   _____

*World History*  Enrichment Activities  **31**

# Enrichment Activity 32

## The Marshall Plan

George C. Marshall's European aid program of 1947, known as the Marshall Plan, was not universally popular. Read the following passage, and use it and the information in Section 1 to respond to the questions that follow.

> Under the Marshall Plan, Western Europe received billions of dollars in economic aid from the United States. Undersecretary of State Dean Acheson articulated the rationale for the plan, declaring that Western Europe was "the keystone in the arch which supports the kind of a world which we have to have in order to conduct our lives."
>
> The terms of the Marshall Plan ensured that the United States would receive an economic return—as well as a political one—on its "investment" in Europe. Legislation establishing the plan specified that all foreign aid dollars received by European nations must be spent on American products in the United States. Despite this stipulation, many conservative Americans denounced the Marshall Plan as a "share-the-American-wealth plan." Meanwhile, liberal critics considered it a "Martial Plan" designed to further the United States' long-term military aims.

1. Interpret Dean Acheson's statement. What did he mean by "the keystone in the arch" and "the kind of a world which we have to have in order to conduct our lives"?

   _____
   _____
   _____
   _____
   _____
   _____

2. Suppose that you lived in the postwar era and followed with interest the formulation of the Marshall Plan. Give your opinion of the plan and support that opinion.

   _____
   _____
   _____
   _____
   _____
   _____

Name ........................................................................... Date ..................... Class ...........................

# Enrichment Activity 33

## The Weight of War

The Vietnam War was one of the most turbulent eras in U.S. history. As the war progressed, so did opposition to American involvement in Vietnam. Yet the soldiers who were fighting in Vietnam often had much more practical concerns on their mind, not the least of which was their own survival. In *The Things They Carried*, Tim O'Brien draws from his own experiences as a soldier in Vietnam. Read the passage, then answer the questions that follow.

The things they carried were largely determined by necessity. Among the necessities or near-necessities were P-38 can openers, pocket knives, heat tabs, wristwatches, dog tags, mosquito repellent, chewing gum, candy, cigarettes, salt tablets, packets of Kool-Aid, lighters, matches, sewing kits, Military Payment Certificates, C rations, and two or three canteens of water. Together, these items weighed between 15 and 20 pounds, depending upon a man's habits or rate of metabolism. Henry Dobbins, who was a big man, carried extra rations; he was especially fond of canned peaches in heavy syrup over pound cake. Dave Jensen, who practices field hygiene, carried a toothbrush, dental floss, and several hotel-sized bars of soap he'd stolen on R&R [rest and rehabilitation] in Sydney, Australia. Ted Lavender, who was scared, carried tranquilizers until he was shot in the head outside the village of Than Khe in mid-April. By necessity, and because it was SOP [standard operating procedure], they all carried steel helmets that weighed 5 pounds including the liner and camouflage cover. They carried the standard fatigue jackets and trousers. Very few carried underwear. . . . Necessity dictated. Because the land was mined and booby-trapped, it was SOP for each man to carry a steel-centered, nylon covered flak jacket, which weighed 6.7 pounds, but which on hot days seemed much heavier. Because you could die so quickly, each man carried at least one large compress bandage, usually in the helmet band for easy access. Because the nights were cold, and because the monsoons were wet, each carried a green plastic poncho that could be used as a raincoat or groundsheet or makeshift tent. With its quilted liner, the poncho weighed almost two pounds, but it was worth every ounce. In April, for instance, when Ted Lavender was shot, they used his poncho to wrap him up, then to carry him across the paddy, then to lift him into the chopper that took him away.

**1.** What was the minimum weight that each man had to carry based on the passage above?

_____

**2.** Are there additional things not mentioned here that you would expect soldiers to bring with them—and add additional weight? What small items might they have carried?

_____

**3.** The variety of items carried by individuals reveals their idiosyncrasies. With so much else to carry, why would someone carry something as heavy as canned peaches?

_____

**4.** Does the way O'Brien described the death of Ted Lavender surprise you? Why or why not?

_____

World History          Enrichment Activities     **33**

Name _____  Date _____  Class _____

# Enrichment Activity 34

## Education for Life

Although contact between European and African cultures often resulted in conflict, many Africans benefited from European forms of education. In the selection below, Senegalese writer and teacher Mariama Bâ (1929–1981) writes to her old classmate, Aissatou, about the influence her education had in forming her ideas of who she would become. Read the passage, then complete the activities that follow. If necessary, use a separate sheet of paper.

Aissatou, I will never forget the white woman who was the first to desire for us an "uncommon" destiny. Together, let us recall our school, green, pink, blue, yellow, a veritable rainbow: green, blue and yellow, the colours of the flowers everywhere in the compound; pink the colour of the dormitories, with the beds impeccably made. Let us hear the walls of our school come to life with the intensity of our study. Let us relive its intoxicating atmosphere at night, while the evening song, our joint prayer, rang out, full of hope. The admission policy, which was based on an entrance examination for the whole of former French West Africa, now broken up into autonomous republics, made possible a fruitful blend of different intellects, characters, manners and customs. Nothing differentiated us, apart from specific racial features, the Fon girl from Dahomey and the Malinke one from Guinea. Friendships were made that have endured the test of time and distance. We were true sisters, destined for the same mission of emancipation.

To lift us out of the bog of tradition, superstition and custom, to make us appreciate a multitude of civilizations without renouncing our own, to raise our vision of the world, cultivate our personalities, strengthen our qualities, to make up for our inadequacies, to develop universal moral values in us: these were the aims of our admirable headmistress. The word "love" had a particular resonance in her. She loved us without patronizing us, with our plaits either standing on end or bent down, with our loose blouses, our wrappers. She knew how to discover and appreciate our qualities.

—From *So Long a Letter* by Mariama Bâ

1. What are some of the happy memories Bâ has of her days at the school?

   _____

2. What benefits did Bâ gain from studying with girls from all over West Africa?

   _____

3. Explain in your own words the headmistress's goals for her students.

   _____

4. How much of an influence do you think education played in shaping Bâ's concept of who she was and what she was capable of achieving? Support your answer with details from the passage.

   _____

5. Pretend you are writing a letter to an old friend about the role that education has played in your life. Is education primarily about learning "facts," or is it about how to live in the world that extends beyond the school? Use examples from your own experience to support your response.

   _____

Name ........................................... Date ........................................... Class ...........................................

# Enrichment Activity 35

## A Single Region, Different Cultures

The Middle East has been an area of conflicts since 1945. Yet many countries of the Middle East have much in common. For example, people in many of the countries of the Middle East speak Arabic. The chart below lists the ethnic groups, languages, and religions of countries in the Middle East. Look at the chart, then answer the questions that follow.

| Country | Ethnic Group(s) | Language(s) | Religion(s) |
|---|---|---|---|
| Turkey | Turks 80%, Kurds 20% | Turkish, Kurdish, Arabic | Muslim 99.8% |
| Syria | Arab 90%, Kurds, Armenians | Arabic, Kurdish, Armenian | Muslim 90% |
| Lebanon | Arab 95%, Armenian 4% | Arabic, French | Muslim 70%, Christian 30% |
| Israel | Jewish 83%, non-Jewish (mostly Arab) 17% | Hebrew, Arabic | Jewish 82%, Muslim 14% |
| Jordan | Arab 98% | Arabic | Muslim 92%, Christian 8% |
| Egypt | Egyptian 90%, Greek, Italian, Arab | Arabic, English, French | Muslim 94% |
| Saudi Arabia | Arab | Arabic | Muslim 100% |
| Kuwait | Kuwaiti 45%, other Arab 35%, Iranians, Indians, Pakistanis | Arabic | Muslim 85% |
| Iraq | Arab 80%, Kurds, Turks | Arabic, Kurdish | Muslim 97% |
| Iran | Persian 51%, Azerbaijani 24%, Kurd 7% | Persian, Turkic, Kurdish, Luri | Muslim 95% |

1. Which country is the most culturally homogeneous—that is, in which country are people most likely to share the same ethnic background, language, and religion? _____

2. Which country has the greatest variety of ethnic groups? _____

3. In which country are the greatest variety of languages spoken? _____

4. In which country is Islam not the religion of the majority? _____

5. Based on this chart, which country would you guess was once controlled by England? Explain your answer.

_____

World History                                                                                                 Enrichment Activities   **35**

# Enrichment Activity 36

## Leaders of Modern-Day Latin American Resistance Movements

Augusto César Sandino, leader of Nicaraguan forces from 1927 to 1933 against United States occupation of Nicaragua, favored strengthening the national economy and getting rid of harmful foreign domination. Emiliano Zapata, Mexican revolutionary leader of the early 1900s, stressed a similar need to strengthen the Mexican economy. Read the quotations from both men below and then complete the activities that follow. Use a separate piece of paper for your answers.

---

. . . [T]he immense majority of Mexico's villages and citizens own only the ground on which they stand. They suffer the horrors of poverty without being able to better their social status in any respect, or without being able to dedicate themselves to industry or agriculture due to the fact that the lands, woods, and water are monopolized by a few. For this reason, through prior compensation, one-third of such monopolies will be expropriated [taken] from their powerful owners in order that the villages and citizens of Mexico may obtain ejidos [communal farmland within a village], colonies, town sites, and rural properties for sowing or tilling, and in order that the welfare and prosperity of the Mexican people will be promoted in every way.

—Emiliano Zapata, announcing his Plan of Ayala, November 28, 1911

---

I believe the state owns the land. . . . I favor a system of cooperatives to work the land.
—Augusto César Sandino

I have also come to understand that men without scruples and without regard for Humanity or God are not above evoking worthy ideals just to achieve their own unworthy goals. In short, from the knowledge I have acquired, I conclude that man can no longer live with dignity if he separates himself from reason and honor.

Because of that belief and also because I can see that the United States of America, with no other right than that derived from brute force, intends to deprive us of our Fatherland and our Liberty, I denounce the unjustifiable threat it poses to our land and sovereignty, and assume before History responsibility for my acts. To remain inactive or indifferent like the majority of my fellow citizens would be to join ranks with those who betray the nation. Thus, my action is justified since my ideas spring from the basic concepts of accepted international behavior.

I respect Justice. I am willing to sacrifice myself for it. Material desires hold no sway over me. The treasures I seek to accumulate are spiritual.

—Augusto César Sandino, 1933

---

1. What social objectives do both men hope to achieve in Mexico and Nicaragua?

2. Would the elites in either Nicaragua or Mexico have supported Zapata or Sandino? Explain your answer.

3. Both Zapata and Sandino were killed by members of their countries' governments. What are the practical benefits to groups like the Zapatistas in Mexico and the Sandinistas in Nicaragua in adopting national heroes such as Zapata and Sandino as their ideological inspirations?

4. Imagine that you are a leader of the Zapatistas in talks with the Mexican government in 1997. Write a statement in which you outline your goals for the people you represent. Be sure to link Zapata's goals with the current goals of the Zapatista movement.

Name _____ Date _____ Class _____

# Enrichment Activity 37

## The War in Bosnia

You have read about the bitter fighting among Serbs, Croats, and Muslims that erupted after the breakup of Yugoslavia and creation of an independent Bosnia. Hundreds of thousands of people were killed and millions were displaced in the fighting. The letter excerpted below was written by a woman in Sarajevo around the time of the Dayton peace talks. Read the letter, then answer to the questions that follow. If necessary, use a separate sheet of paper.

> It's now just 11 p.m., and with small candles which we in Bosnia call "beehives," I'd like to begin a short presentation about myself. I was born in Pale [Bosnia], in the environs of Sarajevo. I spent a happy childhood and youth there, and began a family. I'm 28. I hadn't made much of life but I was proud of what I had up to now. I have an 8-year-old daughter. Her name is Elma; she's finished the first grade. I dreamed of her going to ballet or gymnastics, but now there aren't the conditions for that, since we mostly struggle to survive. We are always in a shelter or in our little room.
>
> I also have a son, Benjamin, who is just 4. He's still too small to know anything, but it's sad that I know he can't go outside and play without a care like children where there is no war. . . .
>
> Before the war, I worked in Pale in a factory. It was a good job and fun, too. Since I've had to leave against my will, I'm without a home, without work and everything that goes with it, but thank God my family and close circle of relatives are still alive. Now everything is directed toward cleaning a small two-bed student room, and raising the children. Because I have some hairdressing skills, sometimes I have a chance to make a few dinars, but that's not even close enough to buy food and clothing. . . .
>
> I used to love corresponding with people, and would write fine, long letters; but now my letters carry a lot of sorrow. I can't write about anything that I love, because when you live in a war, you can only want peace, and I'm tired of living like this. I am a person who loves nature, and especially flowers; but three years is a long time, and most of the time I'm in the room. Please don't reproach me for not writing about music, film and the like; perhaps there will come a time for that. . . .

**1.** How has the writer's life changed since war began?

_____

_____

**2.** What is the tone of the last paragraph? Explain.

_____

_____

**3.** Pretend that the letter is addressed to you. Write your reply.

_____

_____

_____

_____

World History                                   Enrichment Activities    37

# ANSWERS

## Enrichment Activity 1, p. 1
*Answers will vary, depending on the change that students choose and the roles they assume in their ancient societies. Encourage students to use their imaginations and information from the chart and Chapter 1 in their responses.*

## Enrichment Activity 2, p. 2
1. The flooding of the Nile played a central role in the life of ancient Egypt.
2. *Students should infer that building earthen dams and irrigating fields were labor-intensive activities that needed, like the building of the pyramids, an abundant labor force.*
3. Egyptian kings were gods, who were supposed to know and control everything. Their ability to predict was a reflection of their godliness.
4. Land close to the river was flooded more regularly and for longer than more distant fields, making it better for crops and requiring less labor to manage the flooding.
5. Water and the Nile had very important places in Egyptian religion. Water could be provided or withheld as evidence of a god's pleasure or displeasure with the people.

## Enrichment Activity 3, p. 3
*Students may gather a wide variety of possible meanings. Actual meanings of each term are listed below.*

   albacore, fish; algorithm, a set of rules for solving a problem in a finite number of steps; carafe, a bottle for holding liquid; cipher, any Arabic number or figure; garble, mix up; hazard, danger; henna, a kind of dye; lute, a stringed instrument; marabout, hermit; quintal, hundred-pound weight; saffron, pungent yellow spice; saker, falcon; tarragon, a kind of spice

## Enrichment Activity 4, p. 4
1. Chronos and Rhea
2. four; Hera, Demeter, Hades, and Poseidon
3. Hera
4. four; Ares, Hebe, Hephaestus, Triton
5. three; Deimos, Phobos, Harmonia
6. They are first cousins; their fathers are brothers.

## Enrichment Activity, 5, p. 5
1. Cleis, the speaker's daughter; the speaker's beloved
2. It is very loving and protecting; it shows that no worldly value can be placed on Cleis.
3. The speaker admires the man; the speaker wishes to be in his place; the speaker is jealous of the beloved's closeness to the man.
4. One poem expresses the protective love of a parent for a child, and the other expresses a wild, consuming love.
5. *Students' poems will vary but should reflect a style similar to that of Sappho's work.*

## Enrichment Activity 6, p. 6
*United States:*
   Government has three branches: executive, legislative, judicial
   Nearly all adult citizens can vote
   Anyone born in country automatically a citizen; immigrants may seek citizenship
   Executive leader (president) chosen every four years
   Territory has expanded a great deal since republic was founded
   Most powerful military in the world
   Freedom of religion
*Roman Republic:*
   Government had two branches: executive, legislative
   All adult citizens could vote
   Eligibility for citizenship varied
   Two executive leaders (consuls) chosen every year
   Territory expanded a great deal after republic began
   Most powerful military in known world
   Little interference in religion
*Answers will vary, but should reflect an understanding of the strengths and weaknesses of the Roman Republic and the problems it faced during the period of expansion, as well as the basic workings of the United States' government.*

## Enrichment Activity 7, p. 7
1. *Answers will vary. Here is a sample speech:* Members of this council, what can you be thinking? We cannot just move our village to

someplace else. We have lived here for generations. My great-grandfather lived just beyond that hill there. I do not see how moving will help our situation. Instead, I propose that we redistribute the land. The fact that our land yields fewer crops every year can be reversed. We only need allow the land to regenerate itself naturally. We should farm different crops on the land. We can also redirect the flow of the river to bring necessary water to more distant land. That will give us more free land to farm while we leave our current fields fallow. This is what must be done. Moving is only a temporary escape until we unwisely repeat our mistakes in a new area.

2. *Answers will vary. Here is a sample plan:* Following the fourth moon, all shall abandon this village for a new and yet unknown land. The easiest way to travel is to follow the course of the river. The river will guide us to our new country. Teams will be drawn up to make boats so that we can easily transport our heavy belongings. Only valuable possessions should be brought. The most necessary are tools to build new housing, and cooking vessels to prepare food. The elderly, infirm, and children should be brought by boat along the river. Since most of the 100 villagers are strong and able, they should walk along the riverside until suitable new land is found. Enough provisions should be brought to feed the children and elderly. Other food will be gathered along the route. Three teams of ten men shall be formed as protection squads. The teams will take shifts guarding the villagers as they move along the route.

3. One reason that many people move is war. War creates hardship that make families want to leave to find a safe country in which to live. They may move temporarily to a new country until the war is over, or they may move permanently. Often, families choose a new country if they know that they have a friend or relative who has already moved there. The United States is one destination for many people. For example, many El Salvadoran refugees came to the United States during their civil war in the mid-1980s. Many Vietnamese refugees came to the United States for the same reason in the 1970s. About 2 million people living in the former Yugoslavia became refugees. Many of them settled in Germany, Sweden, and other European countries.

## Enrichment Activity 8, p. 8

1. *Possible answer:* They wanted to show off their impressive skills.
2. *Possible answer:* Excessive pride in one's abilities, without practical sense, will lead to disaster.
3. "Ill-Considered Actions," because if the three Brahmans had thought more about the consequences of bringing the lion to life, they would have seen how dangerous it was.
4. *Possible answer:* Fables would be an entertaining way of teaching people how to behave properly in their dealings with local officials and imperial authorities.
5. *Students' fables should be logically organized and illustrate a clear moral.*

## Enrichment Activity 9, p. 9

1. 11 days (29.5 x 12 = 354, 11 days shorter than a 365-day solar year)
2. 30.4 days (365 ÷ 12 = 30.4)
3. about one day (30.4 – 29.5 = 0.9)
4. *Answers may range from 30 to 33.* At about one day per month, it would take 30 months to lose about 30 days. In fact, the leap month is added every 30 lunar months.
5. Because of international trade, it would be difficult to make date conversions constantly, so the Chinese decided to convert to the calendar used by their Western trading partners.

## Enrichment Activity 10, p. 10

1. *Answers may vary. Possible answer:* Eastern Orthodox Populations in Several Countries
2. 10,647,511
3. Armenia, Greece
4. a. 4,351,737
   b. about 6 times
   c. about 11 percent
5. about 25 percent
6. about 6 million

## Enrichment Activity 11, p. 11

*Answers will vary. Possible answers:*
1. The period of fasting is a time of atonement for sins. By fasting, people make themselves more pleasing to God.
2. During Ramadan, the gates of heaven are open and the gates of hell are closed. The physical body is like the gates of hell: it is

"closed" to food; the soul is "open" like the gates of heaven because it is no longer dependent on the body, only on God.

3. The feast of Ramadan places the faithful in the hands of God: every day, people are reminded of their dependence on God for even the most basic necessities of life. Because Muslims believe that God decides the fate of the entire world over the course of a single night, the Night of Determination emphasizes how dependent everyone is on God and His mercy.

4. *It may be difficult for many students to realize how difficult it is to fast for an entire month. Be sure that students understand that no food or drink—not even water—is allowed all day. Additionally, because the Islamic calendar does not correspond to the Julian calendar, Ramadan routinely falls during the summer months when it is most difficult to keep the fast, especially in the hot, dry lands of the Middle East.*

5. Although it is not easy to keep the fast, it is a time of celebration because people are close to their God; because people are undergoing similar hardships, they can support and encourage each other, rather than become discouraged and possibly break the fast.

### Enrichment Activity 12, p. 12

1. *Answers may vary. Students may find they have too many tasks for one day. Encourage them to think of management procedures and time allocation (doing certain tasks every day and some only on certain days) to complete as many tasks as possible. They should discover that managing a household was complicated and required good management skills.*

2. *Lists and locations will vary. Help students to think of the various locations within a castle and its grounds where they might have gathered foods for their meal. Remind them that travel around the estate and to marketplaces was time-consuming and often difficult.*

### Enrichment Activity 13, p. 13

1. *Students may describe the stone walls of the buildings, the people fighting, their weapons, and the bloodshed. There may be screams and cries. Feelings may include anger, exhaustion, fear, bloodthirstiness, and shock.*

2. *Students may mention their own fear, terror, confusion, and despair, the other people running away, the sights of the soldiers, and the cries of those being killed.*

### Enrichment Activity 14, p. 14

1. The Montagnards probably live in a rain forest environment inhabited by exotic animals, such as the toucan. In addition, rice is probably an important staple of their diet since it is represented in so many different patterns.

2. The patterns represent helicopters, guns, and men on horses. They probably represent the intrusion of the Vietnam War and modern technology into the lives of these relatively isolated agricultural people. The patterns may also help explain how widespread the effects of the war were on minority groups in Vietnam.

3. *Students' patterns should be clearly drawn and represent a familiar object. Students should make reference to the importance of preserving information about lifestyles and technology that may become obsolete in 100 years.*

### Enrichment Activity 15, p. 15

1. They thought that history recurred in cyclical patterns and that by understanding these patterns they could create a favorable destiny.

2. *Possible answers:* to interpret Maya history in a way that we can understand today yet is true to the Maya's perceptions of themselves; to reveal the humanity of the Maya.

3. The written history of the Americas begins then with the written records left by the Maya.

4. *Students who answer yes may argue that the Maya contributed to the civilizations that created modern Mexico and Central America. Students who argue no may claim that due to the settlement of the Americas by Europeans and the destruction of indigenous cultures, the Maya way of thought has had little lasting impact on the Americas.*

### Enrichment Activity 16, p. 16

1. The excerpts are describing different groups, but both writings are critical of the wealthy and privileged classes and sympathetic to the poor.

2. *Students may conclude that the commonwealths of the Renaissance are very different from today's societies, stating that the rights of underclasses today are better protected. Or they may*

argue that the systems are, in reality, very similar, stating that the wealthy continue to wield greater power over other classes. Students should provide evidence from the passage and from society today to support their arguments.
3. *Possible answers:* The rich person might argue that his education, skills and abilities, or inheritance entitle him to the fruits of the commonwealth. A poor peasant might argue that his hard, productive work and his care for the land entitle him to the reasonable share of goods that he would receive in a utopia.

## Enrichment Activity 17, p. 17

1. He states that many greater men have been wrong about the existence of the Americas, and he does not wish to commit a similar error.
2. The Europeans see the vastness of the newly-discovered landmass and immediately wish to "consume" or control all it has to offer; unfortunately, this vast richness is too much for the Europeans to handle.
3. Contrary to what others have said or written, Montaigne does not see the inhabitants of the Americas as "savage" or "barbarous"; rather, Montaigne sees them as merely different from Europeans.
4. He thinks the Europeans are too narrow-minded: they assume that what they know is the best way of doing things and therefore do not attempt to learn from other people.
5. *Students should give specific examples to back up their opinions.*

## Enrichment Activity 18, p. 18

1. via the Silk Road through Central Asia and through the coastal areas where ports were located; Muslim communities in China were located around the Silk Road in the northwest portion of the country and in port cities in southern China.
2. During the 1850s the Qing dynasty was weakened by the Taiping Rebellion, leaving it decentralized and vulnerable to further unrest.
3. The Confucian civil service system reinstituted by the Ming and Qing dynasties emphasized loyalty first to the Chinese emperor. Muslims, believers in God, might be viewed as a threat because they chose to obey God's laws or those of a mullah before the laws of the Chinese emperor.
4. Chinese repression of minority religious groups differed markedly from Akbar's religious tolerance, which made life bearable for Hindus and other religious groups as long as they obeyed the Mogul emperor.

## Enrichment Activity 19, p. 19

1. She is there to live or die with the troops.
2. *Answers will vary. Possible answers:* Elizabeth's presence at Tilbury reveals that she is extremely courageous.
3. *Answers will vary. Possible answers:* stirring, passionate, fiery, fervent, emotional
4. *Answers will vary. Possible answers:* It cheered them on, convinced them that their cause was just, and caused them to respect and revere their queen all the more.
5. *Answers will vary. Possible answer:* Philip's speech would be similar to Elizabeth's in tone but would likely be more fiery and urge the Spanish soldiers to show no mercy to the British, because the British are Protestants rather than Catholics.

## Enrichment Activity 20, p. 20

1. *Answers will vary. Possible answer:* Religious dogma keeps us obedient and prevents us from being truly free; Galileo is a heretic and should be condemned.
2. *Ballads, poems, and plays will vary but should reflect that, because their work was controversial in the Church's view, Copernicus worked in secret without publishing and Diderot went to prison.*

## Enrichment Activity 21, p. 21

1. *Answers will vary, but students should focus on the fact that most Americans were strong believers in a "just" government—ruling by the consent of the governed. They believed that people had a right to certain basic freedoms—speech, religion, the press—and also had the right to assemble and address their government for grievances.*
2. *Answers will vary, but students can mention that Washington's ability to command respect and loyalty would only be enhanced by his physical appearance. His control of his dangerous temper may have inspired respect.*
3. *Students could build on Brookhiser's model and mention appearance. Other attributes could*

*include talent, aspects of character (integrity, honesty, loyalty, compassion), and accomplishments.*

### Enrichment Activity 22, p. 22

1. The French army was unable to stem the attacks of the armies of the European monarchies with what was left of the old royal army.
2. *Answers may include that they fought in a less orderly fashion and that they fought for complete victory.*
3. "whereas the prerevolutionary soldiers had been scarce and expensive, the lives of conscripts were plentiful and cheap"
4. *Answers will vary.* France's enemies were monarchies, and they feared the potential threat to their own authority of an armed populace.
5. *Answers will vary, but should be supported with explanations.*

### Enrichment Activity 23, p. 23

1. to trouble-making English and Irish immigrants and their "antagonistic notions"
2. *Answers will vary. Possible answers:* The "twist" was a processing step that was added to the spinners' job. The "sampler" was an inspector hired to examine cotton to see if it was properly worked or of the right quality.
3. Workers resented the "twist," for which they were not compensated, and which slowed them down. They wanted this "drag" discontinued.
4. *Answers will vary, but should present a point of view opposite to that of the treasurer.*

### Enrichment Activity 24, p. 24

1. They love each other; he is respectable; he makes a fine living.
2. She is the youngest of three girls and her older sisters do not have fiancés; her sisters would reject her; her parents would reject her.
3. *Answers will vary, but should take into account both the feelings of the writer and her social and historical context.*
4. No; such a family most likely would not expect a daughter to remain single until her older sisters are married.
5. *Students' letters will vary, but should reflect contemporary social conditions. Students from present-day immigrant families might describe situations very similar to the one outlined in the letter. Conflicts between family expectations and personal desires may appear in the letters of other students as well. Comparisons and contrasts will similarly vary but should recognize ways the problems of today and those of the early twentieth century may be similar even though society has changed.*

### Enrichment Activity 25, p. 25

1. He compares war to a duel and the opponents to two wrestlers.
2. Art and science provide inventions to contend against violence.
3. Clausewitz suggests that international law does not have much effect on preventing violence.
4. Clausewitz defines war as "an act of violence intended to compel our opponent to fulfill our will." *Most students may find it difficult to disagree with this definition, although some students may stress that war is more than merely violence, it is also defined by the destruction and grief that are the result of violence.*
5. *Answers will vary, but should accurately summarize survey results.*

### Enrichment Activity 26, p. 26

*Diagram 1: Northern Italy:* industrial; *Southern Italy:* agricultural; *both:* Italian, Catholic

*Diagram 2: Prussia:* industrial; *Schleswig:* Danish; *Southern German Provinces:* Catholic; *Prussia and Schleswig:* Protestant; *Schleswig and Southern German Provinces:* agricultural; *all three:* German

### Enrichment Activity 27, p. 27

*Answers will vary. Last words should reflect the person's life and/or personality. Possible answers:*

1. Heaven is as glorious as England!
2. This is death, I presume?
3. I am off to establish a powerful new kingdom, bigger and better!
4. There is nothing we cannot conquer with hard work.
5. It's been a bully good ride. Off to another adventure!
6. This is the final indignity. How dare this happen to me!
7. We accomplished great things for China; it is now a modern nation.
8. It was my destiny to expand America's greatness.

9. Viva Free Mexico!
10. Law and order at all costs.

## Enrichment Activity 28, p. 28
1. to American women
2. It is trying to get women to buy government bonds to support the war effort.
3. The homey, maternal look of the woman is an emotional appeal to mothers to support their sons and husbands who have gone off to war.
4. The outstretched hands signify a request, or plea for assistance. Open arms also show giving and generosity.
5. to patriotism, pride, family devotion, heroism, generosity
6. By placing the images in the background, the artist is hinting at the war as a type of reminder of the current situation. If these images were in the foreground, they may have distracted from the main idea and purpose of the poster.
7. *Posters will vary, but should be judged on the directness of the messages and their persuasive effect.*

## Enrichment Activity 29, p. 29
1. a wedding
2. Uncle Sam, who represents the United States
3. foreign entanglements
4. the potential for the League of Nations to involve the United States in foreign entanglements
5. the U.S. Senate
6. According to the Senate, the ceremony is unconstitutional.
7. 1918, at the time of the Paris Peace Conference
8. *Answers may vary. Possible answer:* The cartoonist seems to side with the Senate. The expression "foreign entanglements" has negative connotations, and while the bride looks very determined, the groom looks very scared. The "Senate" is like a hero who arrives to defend the Constitution and to save Uncle Sam.

## Enrichment Activity 30, p. 30
1. *Answers will vary. Possible summary:* The tax on salt affects everyone, especially the poor and the weak, by forcing them to pay a high price on an essential commodity that they could make themselves.
2. It was an obviously unjust law that affected everyone and that was especially hard on the poor and the weak.
3. Despite conflicts among different religious groups, all could be involved in this campaign.
4. The government had stolen something that belonged to the people and made them pay heavily for it.
5. This tactic might have confused and embarrassed the British government, since they would not want to appear to contradict themselves.
6. By exposing the truth—that the government was charging high prices for something that should have been free or very cheap—Ghandi motivated many people to participate in the campaign, thus giving it great force.

## Enrichment Activity 31, p. 31
1. almost twice as costly
2. a. Soviet Union
   b. about 7.5 million
   c. 37.5%
3. a. about 2.85 million
   b. greater
4. World War II
5. a. about 1.36 million
   b. 210,000
   c. because France surrendered to Germany early in the war and thus did not continue to fight them as they did throughout World War I
6. 29.5%

## Enrichment Activity 32, p. 32
1. *Answers will vary. Possible answer:* Acheson saw Western Europe as the region in which the battle against communism must be fought and won; in other words, an important "keystone." For Acheson, communism and freedom could not coexist. He suggested that if the United States permitted Western Europe to remain economically weak and, hence, vulnerable to Communist takeover, Americans could lose the most meaningful aspects of their lives—their economic, political, and social freedom.
2. *Some students may argue that something like the Marshall Plan was essential to preserving democracy in the United States. Other students may raise doubts about the underlying motiva-*

*tions of the Marshall Plan as reflecting U.S. ambitions for dominance and anticipating the cold war with the Soviet Union. Students should support their opinions with evidence.*

### Enrichment Activity 33, p. 33

1. 28.7 pounds
2. *Answers will vary. Possible answers:* There are many things that are not mentioned in the passage, most notably guns and ammunition, which would have greatly increased the weight of what the soldiers carried. Also, many soldiers carried good luck charms, photographs of loved ones, and other personal items.
3. In a stressful and dangerous situation, many people find comfort in familiar things, such as favorite foods, which provide a reminder of "home."
4. *Possible answers:* It is surprising that O'Brien does not seem to be excited or distressed by the death. It is not surprising, because in war death is to be expected. The body of Ted Lavender is only one more thing that the men are forced to carry.

### Enrichment Activity 34, p. 34

*Answers will vary. Possible answers:*

1. Some of her happy memories are the bright colors and order of the school and the feelings of hope she had while living there.
2. The diversity of the girls enriched her education, and she discovered that differences in race and culture were not obstacles to friendship.
3. Her goals were to teach her students to appreciate many different cultures, including their own, and to develop their individual potential.
4. Bâ's education seems to have given her a strong sense of self-worth. Phrases such as "full of hope," "mission of emancipation," "raise our vision," and "discover and appreciate our qualities" help create this impression.
5. *Some students may feel that their education has little to do with how they perceive themselves, while others may acknowledge the great impact that education can have in molding their identities.*

### Enrichment Activity 35, p. 35

1. Saudi Arabia
2. Kuwait
3. Iran
4. Israel
5. Egypt, because English is spoken in Egypt.

### Enrichment Activity 36, p. 36

1. Both hope to use the power of the state to administer justice irrespective of economic class and redistribute land and resources so that the poor can benefit from their use.
2. No, because the elite would be opposed to Zapata's and Sandino's desires for land reform and for granting equal justice to all citizens. Such reforms would jeopardize the economic power of the elite by making them give up their political power or their land resources.
3. Both Sandino and Zapata are famous and popular throughout Nicaragua and Mexico. As men who died for their belief in equality, they appeal to nationalists, who are proud of their country's history. Reformers and poor peasants would be attracted by their revolutionary ideas of land distribution and justice.
4. *Students' essays should be well-organized and refer to concrete examples from the quotations or the chapter.*

### Enrichment Activity 37, p. 37

*Answers will vary. Possible answers:*

1. Before the war, the writer was employed at a job that she enjoyed. She had money and high hopes for her daughter. Since the war began, she has lost her livelihood. Her hopes for her daughter have been reduced by the conditions of war. The writer's daily routine now consists mainly of caring for her young children and cleaning the dormitory room where they live.
2. The tone is sad and apologetic. The writer regrets that she cannot write of things that she loves, such as nature and the arts. She seems worried that her correspondent will find her letters disappointing, but she has some hope times will change.
3. *Students' letters will vary in tone and content but should indicate an understanding of the woman's present circumstances. Call on volunteers to read their completed letters aloud.*